YOUR KNOWLEDGE HAS VALUE

Law and ethics for web designers. The legal and ethical regulation concerning Web Accessibility

Nerea Eschle

Bibliographic information published by the German National Library:

The German National Library lists this publication in the National Bibliography; detailed bibliographic data are available on the Internet at http://dnb.dnb.de.

ISBN: 9783346732392
This book is also available as an ebook.

© GRIN Publishing GmbH
Nymphenburger Straße 86
80636 München

Print and binding: Books on Demand GmbH, Norderstedt, Germany
Printed on acid-free paper from responsible sources.

The present work has been carefully prepared. Nevertheless, authors and publishers do not incur liability for the correctness of information, notes, links and advice as well as any printing errors.

GRIN web shop: https://www.grin.com/document/1280442

Law and ethics for web designer: an essay about the legal and ethical regulation concerning Web Accessibility

Volda University College
Media, Professions and Society

29.10.2021

Table of contents

1. Introduction

The World Health Organization estimates that about 6 to 10 out of every 100 people live with a disability. It is estimated that a total of 135 million people in the European Region have a disability. This number could increase in the coming years as the population ages (WHO Regional Office for Europe). All of these people will most likely face significant barriers when it comes to information and communication technologies (ICTs), such as poorly designed websites where graphics cannot be read by screen readers or information that can only be accessed with a mouse instead of also with a keyboard (Moberly, 2004, cited in Varney, 2013, pp. 1–2). This is fatal at a time when information and communication technologies are becoming increasingly important in our everyday lives. A so-called "digital divide" between people with access to information and those without (Dobransky & Hargittai,2006, pp. 313), could emerge due to rapid technological progress. This potential development makes accessibility such an important issue so that people with disabilities also have full and equal access to information (Varney, 2013, pp. 261). Accessibility is not just about information. It's about enabling people with disabilities to live empowered lives and participate in the online environment where engagement and participation in contemporary politics, culture, and media take place (Varney, 2013, pp. 1–2; Ellis et al., 2015, pp. 9). In thatregard, a change has been taking place since the last decades, and disability is more and more recognised as an important part of society, of the public and private sphere, and daily life. Some of these signs can also be found in the legal sphere: For example, the adoption of the United Nations Conventions on the Rights of Persons with Disabilities (Arnardóttir & Quinn, 2009, cited in Ellis et al., 2015, pp. 8) and various laws and regulations by governments (Francis & Silver, 2000, cited in Ellis et al., 2015, pp. 8). These include Directive (EU) 2016/2102, which requires member states to make public sector websites and mobile apps more accessible. Such new legislation must, of course, be implemented by practitioners. One of these are web designers, as those who create websites (AListApart, 1998, cited in Kennedy,2012, pp. 10). However, little research has been done on professional web designers, particularly the professional ethos and their work (Kennedy, 2012, pp. 10). Therefore, this thesis is dedicated to accessibility laws, voluntary guidelines, and professional regulations andhow they interact with web designers. So the research question asks: How do web accessibility laws and professional codes of ethics affect the web designer's profession and working life? To answer this question, the first part outlines the extent to which web design is a profession and how it has evolved. In the second part, the concept of accessibility, disability, and approaches to accessible design are discussed, then the legal regulations and professional ethics are considered, and finally accessible design in practice. In the end, a conclusion is drawn to summarise the findings and provide an outlook.

2. The development of web design and it's status as profession

To better understand the possible effects of laws and professional ethics on web designers and their work it seems useful to take a step backward to the development of the profession and the question if web design is a profession.

The definition of a profession is very imprecise due to the changing meaning of the term and the changing nature of profession itself, as members of the professions have their own definitions of what they are and what they do (Burrage, 1996, pp. 75). Nevertheless, the various typical characteristics of a profession will be applied below to the profession of web design in order to outline its development. One described characteristic of a profession is that they are "organized bodies of experts who applied esoteric knowledge to particular cases" (Abbott, 1988, pp. 4). What seems to be the focus here is the abstract knowledge that distinguishes the profession from the craft, where the emphasis is more on technique. Building on this emphasis on expertise, a profession is characterised by a particular specialisation. For web designers, the special expertise is to create websites (AListApart, 1998, cited in Kennedy, 2012, pp. 10). This consists of a set of skills that include techniques such as front-end and back-end coding, but also abstract knowledge in the form of user experience and usability design, project management, visual design, information architecture, and digital content management and strategy (Kennedy, 2012, pp. 10). Specialisation was already observed ten years ago when web designers were increasingly seen as a distinct profession, different from amateurs who just do something professionally (Kennedy, 2010, pp. 187). There have also been internal specialisation, whereby a distinction is made between front-end and back-end web designers (Kennedy, 2012, pp. 10).

The second characteristic of the profession is control over the profession itself and the way abstract knowledge is mobilised within the profession, including training and regulation (Abbott, 1988, pp. 4). This includes the fact that professions tend to regulate themselves:

"they set their own standards, establish codes of conduct, set criteria for licensing, discipline members, and so on" (Abott, 1988, cited in Kennedy, 2010, pp. 191). Considering web designers, this criterion seems to be the case in terms of internal standards as well as regulations. Thus, since the first 10 years of its existence as a field of work, the profession has been "normalised": "From its birth as an anarchic free-for-all, web design has undergone a process of standardization, resulting in recognizable job titles, core skills and an emphasis on adhering to the guidelines established by the World Wide Web Consortium (W3C) and other international standards" (Kennedy, 2010, pp. 187). These and other standards were developed by their own experts and resulted in self-regulated web standards to guide web practitioners and good practice (Kennedy, 2011, pp. 93). However, the criterion regarding the education of the profession of web design is not met as this is not standardised or exclusive. Although web designers have a high level of expertise and specialisation, and in theory, this should mean that the work is inaccessible to those who do not have the necessary training and experience, specific formal training is not required. For example, several studies have found that the background of web designers varies widely in terms of degree and field of study: f.e. Computer Science or Information Systems, Media and Communications, Engineering, Administration and Arts (Inal et al., 2019, pp. 390–391; Patel et al., 2020, pp. 3).

A third characteristic of professions, as mentioned earlier, is that they change and can be seen as embedded in "an interacting system, an ecology" (Abbott, 1988, pp. 33). This means that their tasks change and adapt due to new situations such as new competitors or changing system structures. Indirectly, larger social forces can also affect individual professionals through the structure within the professions (Abbott, 1988, pp. 33). In terms of web design, a change can be described that can be attributed to the introduction of accessibility and affects various aspects. For example, the need for accessibility has created new professions such as the "Web Accessibility Specialist" (Rajšp et al., 2019, pp. 95) or the "UX Designer" (Inal et al., 2019, pp. 391). In general, a very large number of job positions in the field of digital accessibility were found (Rajšp et al., 2019, pp. 97; Antonelli et al., 2018, pp. 77). This can be explained, among other things, by the fact that the positions relate to different phases, such as the design, development, evaluation, or conformity testing phase (Rajšp et al., 2019, pp. 95–96). At the same time, existing professions have changed, such as front-end engineers or user interface developers, etc., adapting to the new accessibility standards and technologies.

In conclusion, web design is a profession, even if it does not cover all aspects of the definition. It becomes clear that web design is not a profession in the sense of the professions discussed by Abbott, such as medicine or law, which, unlike the web designer, requireexclusive formal training (Kennedy, 2010, pp. 192). The profession of web design can be better captured by understanding them as part of the media, creative or cultural industries (Hesmondhalgh, 2002, pp. 12, cited in Deuze, 2007, pp. 60). This is possible because the main product websites can also be understood as aesthetic or symbolic (Kennedy, 2012, pp. 10). Such classification helps to categorise other characteristics of the web designer's profession. For example, as a media worker, a web designer must adapt to new demands to a significant degree and does not benefit from the relative stability of a lifelong working style (Deuze, 2007, pp. 10).

3. Disability and the concept of accessibility

The concept of accessibility is based on an understanding of disability as the social creation of unnecessary barriers, exclusion, and discrimination: "One might have a particular impairment, but be 'disabled' or 'enabled' by social arrangements – something reflected in the preferred UK terminology of 'disabled person'" (Ellis & Goggin, 2015a, pp. 78). It is the socialdeterminants, contexts, and dynamics that lead to disability, rather than a medical or health phenomenon. Furthermore, it is important to note that disability can take different forms and also last for different lengths of time. Every person can become more or less "disabled" and could identify with a disability in the course of his or her life. For example, due to age, war, poverty, gender-based violence, working conditions, accidents, and so on (Goggin, 2017, pp. 7). Disability as a social construct is also reflected in web technology. In this case, barriers, obstacles, and inaccessibility have created "built-in" systems rather than "enabling" environments that seek to make technology accessible, usable, and responsive to user's needs and preferences. Disability is consequently something caused by technology, as a result of poor design (Sharp, 2019, pp. 17). To counteract this, an important principle has been developed: "universal design" (Goggin, 2017, pp. 7). Universal design in this context means design that takes into account the widest possible range of people, including differences in gender, income, and education (Sharp, 2019, pp. 17). The idea of universal design is thatwhen designing for disabled users, the end result is a technology that is useful (and accessible) to a wider range of users. An example of this are subtitles in online videos for the deaf or hard of hearing, but also for users in noisy environments or for people who have difficulty understanding the language (Ellis et al., 2015, pp. 11). The overarching goal of universal design is to communicate that accessibility should be an integral part of the design and development of ICT products and services. Central to this is a universalist vision of equality that focuses on promoting the full and equal participation of all citizens in society. Such participation can only be ensured if ICT products and services are designed to adapt to the full repertoire available in society (Varney, 2013, pp. 243). This aspiration is closely intertwined with the idea of the Internet as a globally accessible, universal medium. And in this vision, people with disabilities play a central role (Ellis et al., 2015, pp. 11).

The terms accessibility and usability are often mentioned together in training but also in job descriptions (Ferati & Vogel, 2020, pp. 4; Patel et al., 2020, pp. 3). In fact, accessibility and usability overlap, and thereby accessibility can be seen as a general term for both accessibility and usability (Stienstra & Troschuk, 2005, cited in Varney, 2013, pp. 3; Varney, 2013, pp. 3). The term accessibility refers more to the ability to make information easily accessible in any form, structure, or presentation, regardless of the specific skills of the user (Loiacono et al., 2006, pp. 1, cited in Varney, 2013, pp. 3). Usability, for its part, tends to describe the extent to which a product can be used by users to achieve specific goals with effectiveness, efficiency, and satisfaction in a particular context of use (ISO 9241, 1998). It can be measured in relation to specific users and specific tasks (Nielsen, 1993, pp. 27).

That said, the approach of accessibility of universal design discussed here is also criticised, and therefore its shortcomings will be addressed here as well. One main argument against it is universalisation. By focusing on a universal solution without the need to adapt to specific conditions, some needs may not be taken into account. By this is meant that not everyone interacts with content in the same way, so different options and flexibility should be offered rather than a universal one-size-fits-all solution (Ellcessor, 2018, pp. 111). This seems to be especially true when the needs and expectations of people with disabilities are conflicting or people have a combination of disabilities (Ellis et al., 2015, pp. 11; Goggin, 2017, pp. 5). In addition, the process of universal design is criticised for taking generalised and formulaicsteps rather than considering real feedback from users with specific accessibility needs. To address this, the principle of universal design could be complemented by empirical user testing, where web designers and users interact (Strantz, 2021, pp. 290–291). In this process, the web designer has the opportunity to understand access and adaptation, interventions, and engaged practice (Ellcessor, 2018, pp. 111).

4. Legal obligations about web accessibility: EU-directive

When it comes to internet accessibility, there are a variety of legal and political approaches that can be taken. One of these is the UN Convention on the Rights of Persons with Disabilities (UNCRPD for short) (Lazar, 2019, pp. 248). This emphasises that people "live independently and participate fully in all aspects of life" including the right to access information and communication (Convention on the Rights of Persons with Disabilities,2021). According to Varney (2013), this should lead to the goal of achieving equal access to information, which plays such a central role in the ICT sector (Varney, 2013, pp. 1–2).

There are many different legal regulations and laws at regional, national and internationallevel (Lazar, 2019, pp. 260). As an example for this paper, I would like to briefly discuss the EU Directive. As mentioned in the introduction, the EU Digital Accessibility Directive (EU) 2016/2102 obliges Member States to make public sector websites and mobile applications more accessible. Thus, Article 2 states that Member States may maintain or introducemeasures that go beyond the minimum accessibility requirements for websites and mobile apps set out in this Directive, in accordance with Union law (Publications Office of the European Union, 2018). The aim of this directive is to improve the accessibility of public sector websites and mobile apps and to harmonise the different standards across the EU in order to reduce barriers for developers of accessible products and services. This should enableEU citizens, especially those with a disability, to have better access to public services. Better accessibility in this context means that websites and mobile applications should be improved, especially for people with disabilities, so that they are perceptible, usable, understandable, andstable. However, the EU directive is limited to public sector websites. This distinction can also be found in many national laws (Lazar, 2019, pp. 251).

The impact of legal regulations on actual web accessibility is discussed in the literature. For example, some authors and studies indicate that legal regulations do not make a big difference towards accessibility. For example, a comparative study between the UK as a country with a policy adoption and Indonesia without such showed no significant difference, except that the level of violations of accessibility standards was lower in the UK (Arief et al., 2020, pp. 110–111). Another study result showed that empirical evidence of accessibility benefits can bemore influential than forcing implementation through regulations (Yesilada et al., 2019, pp.6). Another point of criticism is that legal regulations are not effective because they contain too many shortcomings (Palmer & Palmer, 2018, pp. 400). Moreover, companies would do just enough to avoid being sued (Seale et al., 2019, pp. 276). For example, one study showed that whether accessibility is considered depends on, among other things, whether it is a requirement or whether there is any law for it (Antonelli et al., 2018, pp. 78). However, to be truly accessible, it takes more than just meeting the minimum requirement. That said, others point out that legal requirements contribute to a more accessible web design. Several studies have concluded that government and corporate websites put more effort into being accessible because of regulations (Inal et al., 2019, pp. 388; Loiacono & Djamasbi, 2013, pp. 121). In particular, if the knowledge, awareness, and training of responsible persons are low (Ballesteros, 2015, pp. 585), the tendency to consider web design projects may be even lower if accessibility is not supported by government laws and policies (Lazar et al., 2004, pp. 281). In summary, legal regulations can have an impact but do not automatically lead to more awareness or practice of accessible design (Antonelli et al., 2018, pp. 72–73).

5. Professional ethics about accessibility

Apart from the binding legal regulations on accessibility, there are professional ethics. By professional ethics, one understands established normative rules or codes of conduct for a specific profession (Airaksinen, 2012, pp. 618). While it might seem that professional ethics are less influential due to the voluntary nature of following them, the opposite can be observed. The motivation to do the right thing, to act according to professional norms, is oftenhigher than the motivation to comply with legal obligations (Palmer & Palmer, 2018, pp.413). Moreover, the professional ethics reflected in WCAG, a technical standard on web content, are used by governments as components of their laws (Lazar, 2019, pp. 254).

In terms of web design, the movement of web standards seems noteworthy to describe professional ethics. For this reason, the history of web design will be briefly reviewed again at this point. The vision of Berners-Lee, as one of the inventors of the Internet, was an open, interoperable and accessible, and universal medium to which access for everyone was an essential aspect (Berners-Lee, 2003, cited in Kennedy, 2010. pp. 13). This idea, among others, formed the basis for the web standards movement of accessibility initiatives, which influenced young designers with the same ethical ideals. And so web designers who shared the ethos of web standards also tended to employ web accessibility. These individuals have been called the 'standards crowd' and have contributed to the prevalence of this ethos (Kennedy, 2012, pp. 12–13). The aim is to create a more perfect democracy in which the most important normative expectations of democracy - equality, justice, fairness, and the right of each individual to develop his or her individuality - are fulfilled. To achieve this, they are prepared to make the greatest possible effort (Banks, 2007, pp. 186).

One of the most influential guidelines for web designers comes from the W3C, a consortium that aims to ensure the long-term growth of the World Wide Web. The group is made up of practitioners, designers, researchers, and technology leaders from a variety of industries (Strantz, 2021, pp. 291). One of the main goals of the W3C is to make the benefits of the Internet accessible to all people: For people with disabilities, but also for groups such as older people, people in rural areas, and people in developing countries (World Wide Web Consortium [W3C]). To this end, the W3C has launched the Web Accessibility Initiative (WAI), in which working groups develop a framework to guide web developers in creating anaccessible web (Persson et al., 2015, pp. 517). This group developed the Web ContentAccessibility Guideline (WCAG) in its current version 2.0. The developed web standards can be understood as a collection of living documents that evolve and change according to their contributors, including disability groups (WC3, 2021). Such guidelines are widely adopted asthe standard by which a website's accessibility can be measured (Persson et al., 2015, pp. 517).

It is true, however, that guidelines not only offer great potential, as mentioned at the beginning of this chapter but also have certain limitations. Most importantly, guidelines are only voluntary and as such are only used by a few (Palmer & Palmer, 2018, pp. 402; Varney, 2013, pp. 256). The reasons for this are discussed in the following part. However, like universal design, they could serve as a foundation for the creation of accessible web design (Strantz, 2021, pp. 291).

6. Accessible design in practice

After discussing the legal and professional ethics level to understand the working environment of web design, the web designer should be analysed next. In this context,although accessibility has improved since 1999, still the majority of websites fail the WCAG

2.0 standard due to low contrast, lack of alternative text, and others (The WebAIM Million, 2021). This means that accessibility often fails in practice. Therefore, the question arises as to which problems web designers are confronted with. Various observations can be made here. Firstly, the intentions of web designers and students, according to the previously discussed professional ethics, are positive towards a consideration and implementation of accessibility (Kearney-Volpe, 2021, pp. 151). Thus, accessible design is perceived as the right thing to do and the universal web as a goal (Kennedy, 2010, pp. 13). And it could generally be observed that the awareness of web designers is increasing so that more web designers consider accessibility in their projects (Antonelli et al., 2018, pp. 78). However, it should also be mentioned here that there are also internal objections that accessible design limits creativity, inventiveness, and design, while others believe that creativity is mobilised by accessible design solutions (Kennedy, 2010, pp. 194; Ellis et al., 2015, pp. 11). The second important aspect is related to the perceived ability to implement. Studies have identified various aspects of competence and skills for this, such as lack of training in accessibility, practical knowledge,lack of language skills, and training materials (Antonelli et al., 2018, pp. 78). These andothers such as too little control over accessibility decisions (Inal et al., 2019, pp. 396; Putnam,2012, pp. 93) lead to low anticipation and realisation. Third, accessibility may not fit into the way web designers work. Design, in particular, may be seen as a competitive and fast-paced field where they face tight development schedules and pressures, and are only focused on producing a product as quickly as possible without regard to the needs of users (Langdon & Thimbleby, 2010, pp. 446; Lazar, 2019, pp. 247). In addition, web designers may think that users are like themselves, so that, for example, the cognitive requirements of products are too high for people with cognitive disabilities (Langdon & Thimbleby, 2010, pp. 439). Even though many web designers want to include accessibility in their projects, they have to discuss this with stakeholders such as their employer or clients (Shilton, 2018, pp. 147; Putnam et al., 2012, pp. 93). Fundamental and highly influential in this regard is the corporateculture and the extent to which the values of democratization, inclusion, and social justice are embedded, which would support accessibility (Hoover, 2003, cited in Seale et al., 2019, pp.

268). Furthermore, customers and businesses may also present economic, aesthetic, or technical counterarguments (Putnam et al., 2012, pp. 93). The most important seems to be commercial interests and their related fear of higher costs due to the consideration of accessibility in projects (Varney, 2013, pp. 217). And higher costs can arise in a number of places. One of the main factors is time. Implementing accessible design takes time, and also because it is not a "one-time-goal" and a website needs regular maintenance to detect errors innew content (Strantz, 2021, pp. 298; Seale et al., 2019, pp. 267). In addition to lack of time, work overload, further costs, and inadequate tools (Antonelli et al., 2018, pp. 78; Inal et al., 2019, pp. 388) can also be associated with commercial interest.

However, in addition to explicit objections, a lack of knowledge and awareness on the part of organizations and clients can prevent web designers from creating accessible designs. So that accessibility is not considered in projects due to a lack of formal requirements on the part of the organization and a lack of customer requirements (Antonelli et al., 2018, pp. 72–73). Moreover there is no support from management and customers in der Umsetzung (Inal et al., 2019, pp. 388; Patel et al., 2020, pp. 6).

7. Conclusion

The question of this paper was how accessibility laws and professional ethics affect the work and profession of web designers. It became clear that accessibility is changing the profession: Further specialization and new professions are found. With regard to the laws, it was discussed how the work of web designers is influenced. It can be said that laws can increase awareness but alone they do not guarantee the implementation of accessibility in actual projects. The perspective of professional ethics gave an interesting insight that accessibility is very relevant in the field of web design. This can be observed in working practice, where web designers are interested in principle but do not have the capacity (e.g., training, time, tools) and support to do so. One of the main obstacles is the different interests of the company or theclient, also described as the "tension between social and economic value" (Varney, 2013, pp. 3). The social factor is represented here by the human rights and social justice approach,which is in seeming contrast to the economic logic in which accessibility means cost (Varney,2013, pp. 256). In this context, laws can serve as useful tools to strengthen the rights ofpeople with disabilities. Nonetheless, laws should be accompanied by other measures, such asmore and more practical training (Goggin, 2017, pp. 7), more transparency about digital offerings (Lazar, 2019, pp. 257), and encouragement of people with disabilities to become media workers (Ellis & Goggin, 2015b, pp. 95). This list could go on and on; however, that is not what this is about. Rather, it is to highlight the complex ecosystem of web design, in which many different stakeholders come together. One of them is the web designer, who on the one hand is affected by laws and professional ethics, but on the other hand, can create the basis of laws by working on web standards.

This paper attempted to give an overview of web accessibility, further work could focus on specific countries and e.g. make a comparison to figure out to what extent accessibility laws are effective. It might also be interesting for further research to consider how technological developments might affect work in the area of accessible design. In particular, evaluation tools driven by artificial intelligence could bring a lot of potential, as accessibility requirements could be easily checked. This means, on the one hand, that legal compliance canbe checked automatically and, on the other hand, workload reduction for web designers (Lazar, 2019, pp. 257).

References

Abbott, A. (1988) *The System of Professions: An Essay on the Division of Expert Labour.* *Chicago*: University of Chicago Press.

Airaksinen, T. (2012). Professional Ethics. In R. Chadwick (Ed.), *Encyclopedia of Applied Ethics* (pp. 616–623). Elsevier. https://doi.org/10.1016/B978-0-12-373932-2.00080-6

AListApart. (1998). *AListApart.* www.alistapart.com

Antonelli, H. L., Rodrigues, S. S., Watanabe, W. M., & Mattos Fortes, R. P. de (2018). A survey on accessibility awareness of Brazilian web developers. In *Proceedings of the 8th International Conference on Software Development and Technologies for Enhancing Accessibility and Fighting Info-exclusion* (pp. 71–79). ACM. https://doi.org/10.1145/3218585.3218598

Arief, M., Rissanen, S., & Saranto, K. (2020). Effectiveness of Web Accessibility Policy Implementation in Online Healthcare Information. *Studies in Health Technology and Informatics, 270,* 1108–1112. https://doi.org/10.3233/SHTI200334

Arnardóttir, O. M., & Quinn, G. (2009). *The UN Convention on the Rights of Persons with Disabilities: European and Scandinavian perspectives. International studies in human rights: v. 100.* Brill | Nijhoff. http://site.ebrary.com/lib/academiccompletetitles/home.action https://doi.org/10.1163/ej.9789004169715.i-320

Ballesteros, E., Ribera, M., Pascual, A., & Granollers, T. (2015). Reflections and proposals to improve the efficiency of accessibility efforts. *Universal Access in the Information Society, 14*(4), 583–586. https://doi.org/10.1007/s10209-014-0356-1

Banks, M. (2007). *The Politics of Cultural Work.* Springer.

Berners-Lee, T. *Web Accessibility Initiative (WAI) website.* http://www.w3.org/WAI/

Bernhaupt, R., Mueller, F., Verweij, D., Andres, J., McGrenere, J., Cockburn, A., Avellino, I., Goguey, A., Bjørn, P., Zhao, S., Samson, B. P., & Kocielnik, R. (Eds.) (2020). *Extended Abstracts of the 2020 CHI Conference on Human Factors in Computing Systems*. ACM.

Burrage, M. (1996). From a gentlemen's to a public profession: Status and politics in the history of English solicitors. *International Journal of the Legal Profession, 3*(1-2), 45–80. https://doi.org/10.1080/09695958.1996.9960410

Convention on the Rights of Persons with Disabilities. *Article 9 - Accessibility*. United Nations.https://www.un.org/development/desa/disabilities/convention-on-the-rights-of -persons-with-disabilities/article-9-accessibility.html

Deuze, M. (2007). *Media Work. Digital Media and Society Series*. Polity Press. https://ebookcentral.proquest.com/lib/kxp/detail.action?docID=5201384

Dobransky, K., & Hargittai, E. (2006). The disability divide in internet access and use. *Information, Communication & Society, 9*(3), 313–334. https://doi.org/10.1080/13691180600751298

Ellcessor, E. (2018). A Glitch in the Tower: Academia, Disability, and Digital Humanities. In J. Sayers (Ed.), *Media/Cultural studies. The Routledge Companion to Media Studies and Digital Humanities* (pp. 108–116). Routledge.

Ellis, K., & Goggin, G. (2015a). Disability Media Participation: Opportunities, Obstacles and Politics. *Media International Australia, 154*(1), 78–88. https://doi.org/10.1177/1329878X1515400111

Ellis, K. & Goggin, G. (2015b). *Disability and the Media. Key Concerns in Media Studies*. Macmillan Education UK. https://ebookcentral.proquest.com/lib/kxp/detail.action?docID=4762855

Ellis, K., Goggin, G., & Kent, M. (2015). FCJ-188 Disability's Digital Frictions: Activism, Technology, and Politics. *The Fibreculture Journal*(26), 7–31. https://doi.org/10.15307/fcj.26.188.2015

Ferati, M., & Vogel, B. (2020). Accessibility in Web Development Courses: A Case Study. *Informatics*, *7*(1), 8. https://doi.org/10.3390/informatics7010008

Francis, L., & Silvers, A. (Eds.). (2015). *Americans with Disabilities* (0th ed.). Routledge. https://doi.org/10.4324/9781315865737

Goggin, G. (2017). Disability and digital inequalities : Rethinking digital divides with disability theory. In *Theorizing Digital Divides* (ppp. 63–74). Routledge. https://doi.org/10.4324/9781315455334-6

Hesmondhalgh, D. (2002). *The Cultural Industries*. SAGE.

Hoover, S. J. (2003). *IT professionals' response to adoption and implementation of innovations in the workplace: Incorporating accessibility features into information technology for end users with disabilities* [Dissertation, University of Minnesota]. https://search.proquest.com/openview/e0509c3ee131fcd2da6a7621ddb61d24/1?pq-ori gsite=gscholar&cbl=18750&diss=y

Inal, Y., Guribye, F., Rajanen, D., Rajanen, M., & Rost, M. (2020). Perspectives and Practices of Digital Accessibility: A Survey of User Experience Professionals in Nordic Countries. In D. Lamas, H. Sarapuu, I. Šmorgun, & G. Berget (Eds.), *Proceedings of the 11th Nordic Conference on Human-Computer Interaction: Shaping Experiences, Shaping Society* (1–11). ACM. https://doi.org/10.1145/3419249.3420119

Inal, Y., Rızvanoğlu, K., & Yesilada, Y. (2019). Web accessibility in Turkey: awareness, understanding and practices of user experience professionals. *Universal Access in the Information Society*, *18*(2), 387–398. https://doi.org/10.1007/s10209-017-0603-3

International Conference on Software Development and Technologies for Enhancing Accessibility and Fighting Info-exclusion, Aristoteleio Panepistēmio Thessalonikēs,, Association for Computing Machinery., Association for Computing Machinery,, & ACM Digital Library. (2018). *DSAI'2018: Proceedings of the 8th International Conference on Software Development and Technologies for Enhancing Accessibility and Fighting Info-exclusion : June 20-22, 2018.*

ISO-Norm. (1998). *ISO-Normen zur Software-Ergonomie: Richtlinien zur Gebrauchstauglichkeit 9241-11.*

Kearney-Volpe, C. (2021). *Accessible Web Development* [Dissertation]. Steinhardt School of Culture, Education, and Human Development New York City University.

Kennedy, H. (2012). *Net Work: Ethics and Values in Web Design.* https://www.academia.edu/1994457/Net_Work_Ethics_and_Values_in_Web_Design

Kennedy, H. (2011). *Net Work: Ethics and Values in Web Design.* Palgrave Macmillan UK. https://ebookcentral.proquest.com/lib/kxp/detail.action?docID=815892

Kennedy, H. (2010). Net work: the professionalization of web design. *Media, Culture & Society, 32*(2), 187–203. https://doi.org/10.1177/0163443709355606

Lamas, D., Sarapuu, H., Šmorgun, I., & Berget, G. (Eds.) (2020). *Proceedings of the 11th Nordic Conference on Human-Computer Interaction: Shaping Experiences, Shaping Society.* ACM.

Langdon, P., & Thimbleby, H. (2010). Inclusion and interaction: Designing interaction for inclusive populations. *Interacting with Computers, 22*(6), 439–448. https://doi.org/10.1016/j.intcom.2010.08.007

Lazar, J. (2019). Web Accessibility Policy and Law. In Y. Yesilada & S. Harper (Eds.), *Human–Computer Interaction Series. Web Accessibility* (pp. 247–261). Springer London. https://doi.org/10.1007/978-1-4471-7440-0_14

Lazar, J., Dudley-Sponaugle, A., & Greenidge, K.-D. (2004). Improving web accessibility: a study of webmaster perceptions. *Computers in Human Behavior, 20*(2), 269–288. https://doi.org/10.1016/j.chb.2003.10.018

Loiacono, E. T., & Djamasbi, S. (2013). Corporate website accessibility: does legislation matter? *Universal Access in the Information Society, 12*(1), 115–124. https://doi.org/10.1007/s10209-011-0269-1

Loiacono, E. T., McCoy, S., & Romano, N. C. (2006). Information technology systems accessibility. *Universal Access in the Information Society*, *5*(1), 1–3. https://doi.org/10.1007/s10209-006-0018-z

Massimo, R., & Muschert, G. W. (Eds.). (2017). *Theorizing Digital Divides*. Routledge. https://doi.org/10.4324/9781315455334

Moberly, R. E. (2004). The Americans With Disabilities Act in Cyberspace: Applying the "Nexus" Approach to Private Internet Websites". College of Law, Faculty Publications (29) https://digitalcommons.unl.edu/lawfacpub/29

Nielsen, J. (1993). *Usability engineering*. Kaufmann.

Palmer, Z. B., & Palmer, R. H. (2018). Legal and Ethical Implications of Website Accessibility. *Business and Professional Communication Quarterly*, *81*(4), 399–420. https://doi.org/10.1177/2329490618802418

Patel, R., Breton, P., Baker, C. M., El-Glaly, Y. N., & Shinohara, K. (2020). Why Software is Not Accessible: Technology Professionals' Perspectives and Challenges. In R. Bernhaupt, F. '. Mueller, D. Verweij, J. Andres, J. McGrenere, A. Cockburn, I. Avellino, A. Goguey, P. Bjørn, S. Zhao, B. P. Samson, & R. Kocielnik (Eds.), *Extended Abstracts of the 2020 CHI Conference on Human Factors in Computing Systems* (pp. 1–9). ACM.

Persson, H., Åhman, H., Yngling, A. A., & Gulliksen, J. (2015). Universal design, inclusive design, accessible design, design for all: different concepts—one goal? On the concept of accessibility—historical, methodological and philosophical aspects. *Universal Access in the Information Society*, *14*(4), 505–526. https://doi.org/10.1007/s10209-014-0358-z

Publications Office of the European Union. (2018). *Accessibility of public sector websites and mobile apps*. https://eur-lex.europa.eu/legal-content/EN/LSU/?uri=CELEX: 32016L2102

Putnam, C., Wozniak, K., Zefeldt, M. J., Cheng, J., Caputo, M., & Duffield, C. (2012). How do professionals who create computing technologies consider accessibility? In M. Huenerfauth & S. Kurniawan (Eds.), *Proceedings of the 14th international ACM SIGACCESS conference on Computers and accessibility - ASSETS '12* (p. 87). ACM Press. https://doi.org/10.1145/2384916.2384932

Sayers, J. (Ed.). (2018). *Media/Cultural studies. The Routledge Companion to Media Studies and Digital Humanities.* Routledge. https://www.taylorfrancis.com/books/9781317549093 https://doi.org/10.4324/9781315730479

Seale, J., Burgstahler, S., & Fisseler, B. (2019). Tackling the Inaccessibility of Websites in Postsecondary Education. In Y. Yesilada & S. Harper (Eds.), *Human–Computer Interaction Series. Web Accessibility* (pp. 263–279). Springer London. https://doi.org/10.1007/978-1-4471-7440-0_15

Sharp, H., Preece, J., & Rogers, Y. (2019). *Interaction Design: Beyond Human-Computer Interaction.* John Wiley & Sons Inc.

Shilton, K. (2018). Values and Ethics in Human-Computer Interaction. *Foundations and Trends® in Human–Computer Interaction, 12*(2), 107–171. https://doi.org/10.1561/1100000073

Stienstra D., & Troschuk L. (2005). Engaging Citizens with Disabilities in eDemocracy. *Disability Studies Quarterly, 25*(2). https://dsq-sds.org/article/view/550/727/

Strantz, A. (2021). Using Web Standards to Design Accessible Data Visualizations in Professional Communication. *IEEE Transactions on Professional Communication, 64*(3), 288–301. https://doi.org/10.1109/TPC.2021.3091784

The WebAIM Million. *WebAIM: Web Accessibility in Mind.* https://webaim.org/projects/million/

Varney, E. (2013). *Disability and Information Technology: A comparative study in media regulation. Cambridge disability law and policy series.* Cambridge University Press. https://doi.org/10.1017/CBO9781139017947

Vigo, M. (2012). Proceedings of the International Cross-Disciplinary Conference on Web Accessibility. ACM Other conferences. ACM. http://dl.acm.org/citation.cfm?id=2207016 https://doi.org/10.1145/2207016

WHO Regional Office for Europe. *Disability*. https://www.euro.who.int/en/health-topics/Life-stages/disability-and-rehabilitation/areas-of-work/disability

World Wide Web Consortium (W3C). *Why: The case for accessibility*. http://www.w3.org/standards/webdesign/accessibility.

W3C. (2012). *About W3C standards*. https://www.w3.org/standards/about.html

Yesilada, Y., Brajnik, G., Vigo, M., & Harper, S. (2012). Understanding web accessibility and its drivers. In *Proceedings of the International Cross-Disciplinary Conference on Web Accessibility - W4A '12*. ACM Press. https://doi.org/10.1145/2207016.2207027

Yesilada, Y., & Harper, S. (Eds.). (2019). *Human–Computer Interaction Series. Web Accessibility*. Springer London. https://doi.org/10.1007/978-1-4471-7440-0